125 YEARS·ANS
1867-1992

Barbour's

Prince Edward Island Pictorial COOKBOOK

Photographs by Wayne Barrett and Anne MacKay
Text and recipes by Nancy H. George

James-StoneHouse Publications Limited

The Publisher wishes to acknowledge the following for their support and participation, including the provision of recipes: the Province of Prince Edward Island, P.E.I. Department of Agriculture, P.E.I. Department of Fisheries and Aquaculture, P.E.I. Potato Marketing Board, P.E.I. Hog Commodity Marketing Board, P.E.I. Milk Marketing Board, P.E.I. Department of Tourism and Parks, Babineau Fisheries Limited and Rodd Inns. Sincere thanks also to Nancy H. George who compiled the text.

James-StoneHouse Publishing Inc.
P.O. Box 428
Dartmouth, Nova Scotia, Canada
B2Y 3Y5

Text and editing: Nancy H. George and James Gourlay
Design: William Richardson

Canadian Cataloguing in Publication Data
Barrett, Wayne.
        Prince Edward Island pictorial cookbook

        ISBN 0-921128-37-1

1. Cookery, Canadian – Prince Edward Island style * 2. Prince Edward Island – Description and travel – 1981- – Views. * I. George, Nancy H. II. Title.

TX715.8.B38 1992
641.59717   C91-097734-8

Printed and bound in Hong Kong

Cover Photo: Howard's Cove
Title Page: Poverty Beach
Below: Long River
Introduction Page: Canoe Point

CONTENTS

An emerald jewel sits in the Gulf of St. Lawrence. Spectacular beaches are caressed by the Gulf Stream. A patchwork quilt of rich agricultural land surrounded by a bountiful ocean suggests close ties between the land and the sea.

Prince Edward Island, with its magnificent scenery and beaches, provides a relaxed environment in which to live, work and play. Clean air, clean water and fertile red soil combine in the production of high value, high quality products.

The well-tended family farms dominating the countryside, and the surrounding ocean with its picturesque fishing villages, create an ambience and beauty that are the keystones for a strong tourism industry.

The historic capital, Charlottetown, hosted the first talks on Canadian unity in 1864. Scenic walking tours offer the visitor a glimpse of what Charlottetown was like at the time of Confederation.

Islanders take great pride in preserving their heritage through the restoration and renovation of older homes and buildings, not only in the larger centers of Charlottetown, Summerside, Montague, Souris and O'Leary but throughout the whole province.

Top-rated hotels, motels, countr, bed and breakfasts, cottages campgrounds offer the visitor a wide ra accommodations in which to savo special time on Prince Edward Island.

There is no part of Canada in agriculture is a more important com of both the economy and the cu Throughout the year, a variety of fe fairs and exhibitions offer a taste of life and hospitality where visitors home.

Woven into the pastoral life of Edward Island are traditional and inn crafts, created and celebrated in time and present.

Prince Edward Island enjoy reputation as Canada's leading province, responsible for one third Canadian yield, and more than h Canada's seed production. Produce continually making improvements t ever-changing market needs. Island p are sold fresh to consumers, to proc and to farmers all over the world.

The primary cash crop, pot accounts for more than one third of th farm cash receipts, which is more th combined value of all other crops.

ms plant approximately 70,000 acres
oes.

tatoes are by no means the only
dity produced. Dairy products, beef,
sheep, poultry, eggs, cereal grains,
, vegetables, and fruit, as well as
, are also produced. The high quality
nd livestock has led to market
nities at home and abroad.

anada's smallest province is a highly
ialized one where milk is concerned.
85% of the product is processed into
cheese, yogurt and, of course, ice
- *Anne of Green Gables'* favorite treat.

own as the "Kentucky of Canada",
Edward Island features harness
tracks in Summerside and
tetown, as well as a number in rural
f the province, and boasts some of the
t trotting and pacing in Eastern
a.

enic fishing villages embrace the
shores, each one unique. The 1,000-
astline is home to many lighthouses,
breathtaking lookouts with endless
raphic opportunities.

land fishermen harvest from the
ant fishing grounds of the Gulf of St.
nce, the Northumberland Strait,

inshore bays and estuaries. Many inshore
fishermen engage in the lucrative lobster
fishery, which accounts for much of their
annual income.

"Malpeque" oysters from Prince Edward
Island have long been recognized by
connoisseurs as the finest available. The
name is taken from one of the more
productive oyster-rearing bays, but is
applied to all oysters produced in the
province.

"Island Blue" mussels, with their sweet
delicate taste, have become extremely
popular among seafood lovers. Cultured
mussels receive extra care and attention
and, as a result of they way they are grown,
are free of grit and full of meat.

Along with the major processed
products, Island entrepreneurs add their
special touches to the best from land and
sea to provide truly unique products which
can be found in specialty shops throughout
North America.

The combination of land, sea and
culture creates an environment to make
Prince Edwards Island, truly, "One of the
World's Great Islands".

Prince Edward Island POTATOES

From our Rich Red Garden to you

The Prince Edward Island Potato-unexcelled quality, taste and variety to enhance any potato recipe.

POTATOES

The first record of potato production in Prince Edward Island comes from a 1771 report sent by the colonial governor to England. In the report, the year's potato crop is described as a "phenomenal success". By 1790, Island farmers were exporting small quantities of potatoes to Nova Scotia and New Brunswick, and by 1830 to the West Indies. In fact, because of the nature of transportation at that time and the poor quality of the roads, it was actually easier and cheaper for some farmers to ship their potatoes to the West Indies via local ports than to get them to Charlottetown.

Today the potato is the world's fourth largest food crop. One reason for this popularity is its high food value - the potato can produce more food energy and protein per hectare than any other food crop except sugar and soybeans, respectively. Potatoes are high in nutrients, low in fat content and contain a good balance of the eight essential amino acids in their protein. They are also economical and easy to prepare in many ways.

Potato varieties have changed over the years as the demand for seed, tablestock and processing potatoes change. The most popular variety of potatoes is the Russet Burbank, which has very high cooking and keeping qualities. It is the leading variety in Canada for french fries and is also outstanding for baking. Other varieties grown include Kennebec, Superior, Sebago, Red Pontiac, Norchip, Shepody, Green Mountain, Atlantic, Yukon Gold and Bintje.

PEI POTATO, CHICKEN AND CORN CHOWDER

A delicious soup, easily made and virtually fat free.

2 cups	chicken stock	500 mL
1/2 cup	onion, chopped	125 mL
1 cup	celery, chopped	250 mL
1/2 cup	carrot, finely chopped	125 mL
2 cups	**PEI Potatoes,** peeled and diced	500 mL
1	can (19 oz/540 mL) creamed corn	1
2 cups	cooked chicken cut into bite-size pieces	500 mL
1 cup	milk	250 mL
	Salt and pepper, to taste	

In large saucepan or Dutch oven, combine chicken stock, onion, celery, carrot and potatoes. Bring to a boil, simmer 15 -20 minutes until vegetables are tender. Add corn, chicken, milk and seasonings. Heat, but do not boil. Makes 6 servings.

Microwave Instructions:
In deep 3 qt (3 L) microwave safe bowl or casserole, combine chicken stock, onion, celery, carrots and potatoes. Microcook covered on HIGH (100%) 12 - 15 minutes, until vegetables are tender. Add corn, chicken and milk. Season to taste. Microcook on HIGH (100%) 3 -5 minutes or until hot. Makes 6 servings.

Tip: To de-fat homemade chicken broth, refrigerate cooked broth until cold, fat will solidify on surface and can easily be removed with a spoon.

Photo: Potato Farm, Knutsford

LUSCIOUS FILLED PEI POTATOES

As good as it looks! Baked potato, mashed; filled with vegetables and piled back into the potato skin.

1	large (8 oz/227 g) **PEI Potato,** baked	1
2-3 tbsp	milk	25-45 mL
1/4 cup	cottage cheese	50 mL
2 tbsp	toasted sunflower seeds	25 mL
2 tbsp	green pepper, chopped	25 mL
2 tbsp	carrot, finely chopped	25 mL
2 tbsp	green onion, sliced	25 mL
1/4 cup	Cheddar cheese, shredded	50 mL
	Salt to taste	
1/8 tsp	pepper	0.5 mL
	Tomato slices	

Halve and scoop out potato, leaving 1/4" (6 mm) pulp in shells. Mash potato; add milk, cottage cheese, sunflower seeds, green pepper, carrot, green onion, half the Cheddar cheese, salt and pepper. Blend gently. Mound into potato shells; arrange tomato slices on each. Sprinkle with remaining cheese. Bake in 450°F (230°C) oven about 10 minutes until cheese is melted and potatoes are heated through. Makes 2 servings.

Tip: Potatoes may be prepared ahead of time. Wrap securely and refrigerate up to 2 days or freeze. These may also be microwaved.

PEI POTATO SALAD AND HAM LOAF

A natural for summertime entertaining - this attractive and delicious molded salad is easy to make.

7-8	medium-size **PEI Potatoes,** peeled and cooked	7-8
1/4 cup	cider vinegar	50 mL
2 tbsp	olive oil	25 mL
	Salt and pepper, to taste	
1 cup	thinly sliced celery	250 mL
1/4 cup	chopped dill pickles	50 mL
1/4 cup	chopped pimento	50 mL
3/4 cup	salad dressing	175 mL
1 tbsp	Dijon mustard	15 mL
3/4 lb	ground cooked ham	350 g
	Green onion	
	Tomato, cut in eighths	
	OR	
	Hard-cooked egg slices	

Place potatoes while still hot, in a large bowl; chop coarsely. Sprinkle hot potatoes with vinegar, oil, salt and pepper to taste. Toss gently to coat; stir in celery, dill pickles and pimento. In small bowl, mix salad dressing and mustard. Gently stir into potato mixture. Line a 9" x 5" (2 L) loaf pan with wax paper. Press 1/3 of the potato mixture into pan. Top with 1/2 of the ham, packing firmly. Repeat layers ending with potato salad. Cover and chill overnight. To serve, unmold onto lettuce-lined platter, peel off wax paper. Garnish with green onion tops and tomatoes or egg slices, if desired. Cut into slices to serve. Makes 6 to 7 servings.

Photo: Cavendish

11

PEI POTATO BANNOCK

Bannock dates back to Prince Edward Island's early settlers. This updated version has added wheat germ for fiber and mashed potato to keep the bannock moist longer.

2 1/4 cups	all-purpose flour	550 mL
1/3 cup	wheat germ	75 mL
4 tsp	baking powder	20 mL
1/2 tsp	baking soda	2 mL
2 tbsp	brown sugar	25 mL
1/2 tsp	salt	2 mL
1/4 cup	soft butter	50 mL
1/2 cup	raisins	125 mL
1 cup	milk	250 mL
1/2 cup	warm, mashed	125 mL
	PEI Potato	

Blend together flour, wheat germ, baking powder, soda, brown sugar and salt in mixing bowl. Cut in butter until mixture has consistency of corn meal. Stir in raisins. Whip potato and milk together until no lumps remain. Make a well in centre of dry ingredients; add the potato-milk mixture. Stir gently with a knife. Turn dough onto lightly floured board; knead for few seconds. Pat into a circle 6-7" (15-18 cm) in diameter and 1" (2.5 cm) thick. Place on lightly greased baking sheet. Bake in 425°F (220°C) oven for about 25 minutes or until lightly browned. Cut in wedges and serve warm. Makes 8 servings.

FLUFFY PEI POTATOES WITH LEEKS

Melt-in-your-mouth mashed potatoes, with a difference.

1/2 cup	chopped green onion	125 mL
2 - 3 tbsp	chopped leek	25 - 45 mL
3/4 cup	milk	175 mL
4	medium-sized **PEI Potatoes,** peeled, cooked, and mashed	4
2 tbsp	butter	25 mL
1/4 tsp	salt	1 mL
1/4 tsp	pepper	1 mL

In saucepan, combine the leek, milk and all but 1 tbsp (15 mL) of green onion. Simmer over medium heat. Cook for 15 minutes or until softened. Set aside. To potatoes, beat in butter and enough hot milk mixture to make creamy potatoes. Be sure to use all the leek and onion. Season with salt and pepper. Garnish with remaining green onion. Makes 4 - 5 servings.

Photo: West River

Prince Edward Island, The Garden of the Gulf

P.E.I. DEPARTMENT OF AGRICULTURE

SCALLOPED PEI POTATOES WITH CABBAGE AND ONIONS

A flavorful, hearty casserole that is bound to please your family.

4	slices bacon, diced	4
2 cups	shredded cabbage	500 mL
2	onions, chopped	2
4	**PEI Potatoes**, peeled and thinly sliced Rosemary, salt and pepper, to taste	4
2 tbsp	butter	25 mL
2 tbsp	all-purpose flour	25 mL
1 1/2 cups	chicken stock	375 mL

In casserole, microcook bacon 4 minutes on HIGH (100%) or until crisp, stirring after 2 minutes. Remove bacon and set aside. Add cabbage and onions to casserole and microcook 4 minutes on HIGH (100%) or until cabbage is wilted, stirring after 2 minutes. In lightly greased 6 cup (1.5 L) casserole, layer potatoes and cabbage-onion mixture. Season each layer with cooked bacon, rosemary, salt and pepper. In bowl, melt butter. Stir in flour; gradually add chicken stock, stirring constantly. Microcook for 2-3 minutes on HIGH (100%) or until sauce bubbles and thickens, stirring after 2 minutes. Pour over vegetables. Microcook 25-30 minutes on HIGH (100%) turning dish a 1/4 turn every 5 minutes until potatoes are tender. Garnish with paprika if desired. Makes 5 - 6 servings.

Tip: May also be baked in a 350°F (180°C) oven for 45-60 minutes or until potatoes are tender.

*Photo: Harvesting Potatoes
North Lake*

15

FESTIVE PEI POTATO CHOCOLATE CAKE

For that special touch, try this moist and delectable potato-based dessert. Serve with your own favorite frosting, or boiled icing topped with coconut.

1/2 cup	butter	125 mL
2 1/4 cups	brown sugar, firmly packed	550 mL
1/2 cup	**PEI Potato,** mashed at room temperature	125 mL
3	squares unsweetened chocolate, melted	3
3	eggs	3
2 3/4 cups	sifted cake flour	675 mL
2 tsp	soda	10 mL
1/2 tsp	salt	2 mL
1/2 cup	milk, soured	125 mL
1 tsp	vanilla	5 mL
1 cup	boiling, clear potato water	250 mL

Cream butter and sugar until light and fluffy. Beat in mashed potato and chocolate. Add eggs, one at a time, beating well after each addition. Sift cake flour, measure, then add soda and salt and sift again. Beat dry ingredients into creamed mixture, alternately with soured milk (to sour, stir into milk, 1 1/2 tsp / 7 mL lemon juice or vinegar and let stand a few minutes). Add vanilla. Gently stir in hot potato water (batter will be very thin). Pour batter into greased and floured l9" (23 cm) angel food or bundt pan; or 13" x 9" (33 x 22 cm) pan. Bake in 350°F (180°C) oven 55 to 60 minutes for angel food or bundt pan; or 40 to 45 minutes for oblong pan. Cool 10 to 15 minutes before removing from pan.

Microwave Instructions:
Prepare cake batter as above. Thoroughly grease a microwave 12 cup (3 L) bundt pan. Microcook on MEDIUM (50%) 10 minutes then on HIGH (100%) 6 to 7 minutes, turning cake 1/4 turn every 3 to 4 minutes. The cake is done when a toothpick scratching the surface of the top shows a dry texture beneath. Let cake stand 15 minutes before removing from pan.

Photo: New Haven

PEI POTATO FUDGE
Creamy and delicious, this traditional favorite is sure to be a hit.

5	squares semi-sweet chocolate	5
1/4 cup	butter	50 mL
2/3 cup	hot, mashed **PEI Potatoes**	150 mL
pinch	salt	pinch
1 tsp	vanilla	5 mL
4-5 cups	icing sugar	1-1.25 L
1/2 cup	chopped nuts	125 mL

Put chocolate and butter in a large bowl. Microcook on MEDIUM (50%) for 2 to 3 minutes or until melted, stirring once. Add potatoes, salt and vanilla. Whisk or stir well. Gradually stir in icing sugar until smooth and desired consistency is reached. Stir in nuts. Spread into greased 9" x 9" (2.5 L) pan. Cool and cut into squares.

Photo: Wood Islands

17

PARTY PEI POTATO CASSEROLE

Cooked potatoes, cubed, or frozen PEI hash browns are the basis of this delicious make-ahead casserole.

6	slices, bacon cut in 1/2" (1 cm) pieces	6
1/2 cup	onion, chopped	125 mL
1 cup	dairy sour cream	250 mL
1/2 cup	mayonnaise	125 mL
1	can (10 oz/284 mL) undiluted mushroom soup	1
1 cup	shredded Cheddar cheese	250 mL
1	can (10 oz/284 mL) sliced mushrooms, drained	1
1/2 tsp	salt	2 mL
	Pepper	
6	medium-size cooked **PEI Potatoes**, diced or	6
1	pkg (1.65 lb/750 g) hash browns	1
1	can (10 oz/284 mL) water chestnuts, drained and sliced	1
1 cup	crushed potato chips (optional) Paprika	250 mL

Microcook bacon in shallow casserole on HIGH (100%) 6 to 7 minutes or until crisp. With slotted spoon remove bacon and drain off fat. Add onion to casserole and microcook on HIGH (100%) 1 to 2 minutes or until tender. In large bowl, mix sour cream, mayonnaise, soup, cheese, mushrooms, salt and pepper. Stir in bacon and onion. Fold in potatoes and water chestnuts. Blend well. Spoon into 3 qt (3 L) or 9" x 13" (23 x 33 cm) buttered dish. Microcook on HIGH (100%) 10 minutes. Stir; add potato chips as a topping if desired. Sprinkle with paprika. Microcook on HIGH (100%) 5 to 10 minutes. Makes 10 to 12 servings.

Photo: North Rustico

18

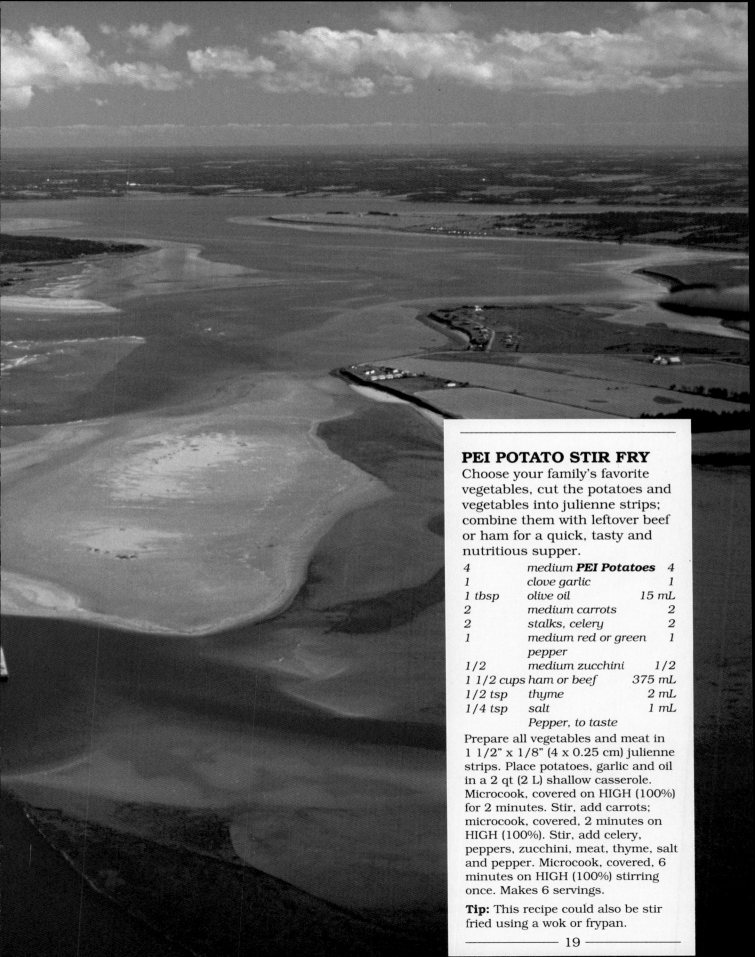

PEI POTATO STIR FRY

Choose your family's favorite vegetables, cut the potatoes and vegetables into julienne strips; combine them with leftover beef or ham for a quick, tasty and nutritious supper.

4	medium **PEI Potatoes**	4
1	clove garlic	1
1 tbsp	olive oil	15 mL
2	medium carrots	2
2	stalks, celery	2
1	medium red or green pepper	1
1/2	medium zucchini	1/2
1 1/2 cups	ham or beef	375 mL
1/2 tsp	thyme	2 mL
1/4 tsp	salt	1 mL
	Pepper, to taste	

Prepare all vegetables and meat in 1 1/2" x 1/8" (4 x 0.25 cm) julienne strips. Place potatoes, garlic and oil in a 2 qt (2 L) shallow casserole. Microcook, covered on HIGH (100%) for 2 minutes. Stir, add carrots; microcook, covered, 2 minutes on HIGH (100%). Stir, add celery, peppers, zucchini, meat, thyme, salt and pepper. Microcook, covered, 6 minutes on HIGH (100%) stirring once. Makes 6 servings.

Tip: This recipe could also be stir fried using a wok or frypan.

Edouard Babineau preparing award-winning recipe, Lobster Crêpes (page 28)

BABINEAU'S

Babineau Fisheries Limi
Morell
Prince Edward Island
Canada   C0A 1S0
Telex No. 014 44252

LOBSTER

Lobster fishing has been a way of life on Prince Edward Island for more than a century. Its importance to the Island has never been greater than it is today.

As they did many years ago, fishermen make their daily journey, spring and fall, to the nearby lobster grounds where they haul the traps which catch the lobster on the seabed.

During the past decade, effective stock management programs have provided a greater harvest potential than ever before, while leaving abundant lobster stocks for the future. Aided by modern processing, storage and transportation methods, the increased harvest is transformed into the finest seafood and delivered to your table.

For the uninitiated, a Prince Edward Island lobster dish opens the door to a whole new world of dining delight. For those familiar with this unique eating experience, it represents a meal that is frequently described in a single phrase.... distinctly delicious.

This delectable seafood from clear, cold Atlantic waters offers even more. It's high in protein and low in fat. Island lobster is available live, freshly cooked in the shell or packed in vacuum pouches or cans.

The versatility of this gourmet seafood is unsurpassed. Served by itself or as the main ingredient in dishes such as chowders or casseroles, you can create a main course that would make any chef proud.

COOKING LIVE LOBSTER

Island Lobsters are distinctly delicious. The best method to cook lobster is by boiling. Fill a large pot with enough salted water (2 tbsp/25 mL of salt per quart/litre of water) to completely cover the lobsters.

Bring the salted water to a boil. Grasp the lobster firmly by the back just behind the claws and plunge it head-first into the boiling water. Cover the pot and let it return to the boil. Start timing as soon as the water returns to the boil.

Depending on the size, lobster will cook in 16 - 21 minutes. Use the following table as a guide.

Weight	Cooking Time	Weight
3/4 lb	16 mins	375 g
1 lb	17 mins	500 g
1 1/2 lbs	19 mins	750 g
2 lbs	21 mins	1 kg

To seal in the juices, as soon as the lobsters are cooked, plunge them into salted ice water for about 3 minutes, then remove and place them on their backs on a tray to drain.

All the lobster is edible except for the shell, the small stomach (hard sac) behind the head, and the dark vein running down the back of the tail. The green material in the body is the liver or tomalley and the red material is the roe, which is found in the body of the female lobster. The tomalley and the roe may be eaten in moderation.

Photo: New London
(Left) Lobster Traps, Sea Cow Pond

FESTIVE SEAFOOD CHOWDER

A creamy, flavorful melody of seafoods.

2 cups	**PEI Lobster** meat	500 mL
1 lb	**PEI Cod** fillets	500 g
1 cup	water	250 mL
1 lb	**PEI Clams** or	500 g
	Island Blue Mussels,	
	steamed and shucked	
1/4 cup	butter	50 mL
1/2 cup	chopped onions	125 mL
2 tbsp	flour	25 mL
4 cups	potatoes, peeled	1 L
	and diced	
4 cups	cream or half & half	1 L
3 cups	milk	750 mL
2 tsp	salt	10 mL
pinch	white pepper	pinch
pinch	cayenne pepper	pinch

If frozen, thaw lobster; drain and reserve lobster liquid. Remove any bits of shell or cartilage. Cut into bite-size pieces. Simmer cod in water for 10-12 minutes. Remove and reserve the cooking liquid. Flake the cod. Leave the clams or mussels whole.

In a heavy saucepan, melt butter and sauté onions until tender. Stir in flour and cook 1 minute. Add potatoes and enough water to barely cover them. Bring to a boil and cook until tender, stirring once or twice. Add cream or half and half, milk, lobster, lobster liquid, cod, cod liquid and clams or mussels. Heat gently and season to taste. Makes 12 servings.

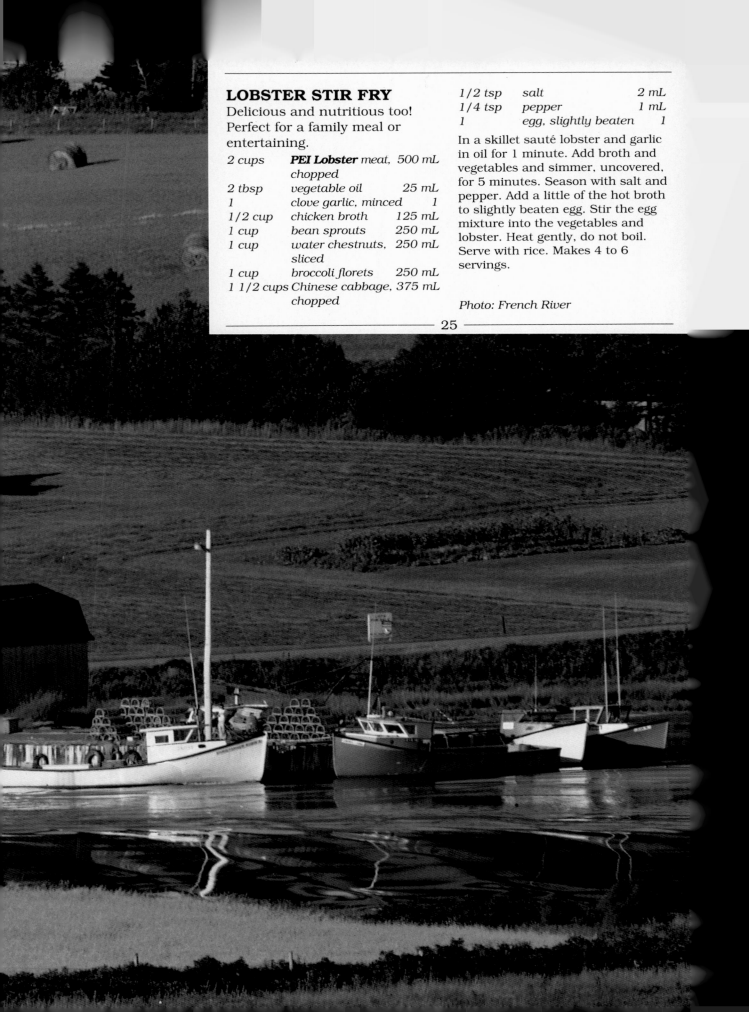

LOBSTER STIR FRY

Delicious and nutritious too! Perfect for a family meal or entertaining.

2 cups	**PEI Lobster** meat, chopped	500 mL
2 tbsp	vegetable oil	25 mL
1	clove garlic, minced	1
1/2 cup	chicken broth	125 mL
1 cup	bean sprouts	250 mL
1 cup	water chestnuts, sliced	250 mL
1 cup	broccoli florets	250 mL
1 1/2 cups	Chinese cabbage, chopped	375 mL
1/2 tsp	salt	2 mL
1/4 tsp	pepper	1 mL
1	egg, slightly beaten	1

In a skillet sauté lobster and garlic in oil for 1 minute. Add broth and vegetables and simmer, uncovered, for 5 minutes. Season with salt and pepper. Add a little of the hot broth to slightly beaten egg. Stir the egg mixture into the vegetables and lobster. Heat gently, do not boil. Serve with rice. Makes 4 to 6 servings.

Photo: French River

25

LOBSTER ROLLS

The rich taste of lobster and cheese on crusty rolls, hot from the oven.

2 cups	**PEI Lobster** meat	500 mL
2 tbsp	celery, diced	25 mL
1 tbsp	onion, chopped	15 mL
1/4 cup	salad dressing	50 mL
1 tsp	lemon juice	5 mL
6	rolls	6
1/4 cup	Cheddar cheese, grated	50 mL

Cut lobster into bite-size chunks and combine with celery, onion, salad dressing and lemon juice. Split rolls in center and fill with lobster mixture. Sprinkle with Cheddar cheese and broil in oven until cheese melts and mixture is heated (about 5 minutes) or microcook on HIGH (100%) about 2 minutes, until hot. Makes 6 servings.

Photo: Cove Head

LOBSTER SCRAMBLE

Quick and easy, a real treat at lunch time.

1 cup	**PEI Lobster** meat	250 mL
8	eggs	8
dash	salt and pepper	dash
1/3 cup	milk, cereal cream, or half and half	75 mL
2 tbsp	butter	25 mL
	Parsley	

Drain lobster; remove any cartilage; cut into bite-size pieces. In a bowl, beat eggs until frothy, season with salt and pepper. Add milk, cereal cream, or half and half. Melt butter in a skillet, add lobster stirring until heated. Pour egg mixture over lobster and stir until cooked. Serve on toast and garnish with parsley. Makes 6 servings.

PRINCE EDWARD ISLAND LOBSTER CREPES

A prize winner from Babineau Fisheries Limited.

Creamy Lobster Filling

2	cans (11.3 oz/320 g) **PEI Lobster** meat, chopped	2
1/4 cup	butter	50 mL
2 tbsp	chopped onion	25 mL
1 cup	chopped mushrooms	250 mL
1/4 cup	all purpose flour	50 mL
1/2 tsp	salt	2 mL
dash	pepper	dash
1 cup	milk	250 mL
1/4 cup	butter, melted	50 mL
1 cup	grated Swiss cheese	250 mL

Sauté onion and mushrooms in 1/4 cup (50 mL) of melted butter for 3-5 minutes. Stir in flour and seasonings, add milk and cook, stirring constantly until thickened. Add lobster, then spoon filling into crêpe, roll up and arrange on baking sheet. Brush with remaining melted butter, add white sauce (optional) and sprinkle with grated cheese. Bake at 425°F (220°C) for 5 - 8 minutes. Makes 4 servings.

Crêpes

3	eggs	3
1 1/4 cups	all purpose flour	300 mL
3/4 tsp	salt	4 mL
1 1/2 tsp	dried parsley	7 mL
1 2/3 cups	milk	400 mL

Beat eggs, add flour and seasonings. Add milk, beat until smooth. Refrigerate for 2 hours. Pour 1/3 cup (75 mL) of mixture into crêpe pan or well-oiled pan and brown lightly on each side. Stack in waxed paper.

White Sauce (Optional)

3 tbsp	butter	45 mL
3 tbsp	flour	45 mL
1 cup	milk	250 mL

Melt butter in a pan over medium heat. Stir in flour, then milk. Heat until thickened. Pour over each crêpe before adding Swiss cheese.

LOBSTER MOUSSE

This lighter version uses milk as a base for a truly Island taste-tempter. Special as an appetizer salad plate or equally delicious served with crackers or melba toast for a snack or before-dinner treat.

1	envelope unflavored gelatin	1
1 cup	milk	250 mL
1/2 cup	plain yogurt	125 mL
1/4 cup	green onions, finely chopped	50 mL
1/3 cup	celery, finely chopped	75 mL
1 tbsp	lemon juice	15 mL
3 tbsp	fresh parsley, chopped	45 mL
1/2 tsp	salt	2 mL
1	garlic clove, minced	1
3 tbsp	ketchup	45 mL
2-3	drops tabasco sauce	2-3
	Pepper, to taste	
1 cup	**PEI Lobster**, meat coarsely chopped	250 mL
2 tbsp	lobster juice	25 mL

In small saucepan or microwave-safe bowl, sprinkle gelatin over milk; let stand about 5 minutes. Warm over medium heat until dissolved or microcook on High (100%) for 1 1/2 minutes. Stir in remaining ingredients, mixing well. Pour into lightly oiled 4 cup (1 L) mold or bowl. Cover and refrigerate several hours or overnight, until firm. To unmold, loosen edges with a knife and dip mold in warm water for a few seconds. Invert onto serving plate; hold mold and plate securely and give a strong shake to release mousse. Remove mold and garnish with parsley or lemon slices. Makes about 3 1/2 cups (875 mL).

Photo: Gaspereaux

Prince Edward Island Milk Marketing Board

MILK

Although milk has been with us throughout history, Prince Edward Island's modern dairy industry has adapted to consumers' wishes for convenience, taste, and simplicity. Milk products have many faces — cheese, yogurt, butter, and ice cream — the favorite of Anne of Green Gables.

Have you ever wondered about the path that milk takes to get to your table? It takes from two to four days to get from the cow to your refrigerator. During this time, the milk is not touched by human hands. The complicated process involves dairy farms, tanker trucks, huge refrigerators, pasteurizers and packages. A good dairy cow could produce enough milk to give you more than 80 glasses or 20 litres each day.

No other beverage boasts the nutritional content of milk. It is an excellent source of high-quality protein, calcium, riboflavin and vitamin D for all ages.

Be you seven or 70, living in the city or the country, looking for quick meals, feeding a family or entertaining friends, versatile milk and milk products will keep pace with your needs every day of the week.

Milk will make soups creamier, sauces smoother, casseroles moister, and desserts that will be the highlight of any gathering. The ways to cook with milk are endless — custards and puddings, sauces and toppings, casseroles and pasta dishes. And of course, it is always good served as a beverage on its own — hot or cold.

MARVELOUS MILK DRINKS

FRUIT FLIP

Let your imagination be your only guide in creating refreshing milk mixtures using either Island fresh or frozen fruit ... strawberries and raspberries are especially marvelous!

1 cup	**PEI Milk**	250 mL
1/2 cup	plain yogurt	125 mL
2 cups	fresh or frozen fruit	500 mL
4	large ice cubes	4

Place ingredients in blender; cover and blend until smooth. Makes 4 servings.

CAFE AU LAIT

This smooth, heartwarming drink is best when the coffee and milk are the same temperature. Heating the milk in the microwave is a time saver.

1 1/2 cups hot **PEI Milk**	375 ml
1 1/2 cups strong hot coffee	375 ml
	sugar to taste
	cinnamon

Pour equal amounts of hot milk and coffee simultaneously into each cup. Stir in sugar, to taste, if desired and sprinkle with cinnamon. Makes 4 servings

Photo: Ayrshire Cows, Fredericton

BROCCOLI CAULIFLOWER DELUXE

This taste-tempting casserole can be prepared early in the day and heated just at mealtime.

2 cups	fresh or frozen broccoli florets	500 mL
2 cups	fresh or frozen cauliflower florets	500 mL
1/4 cup	butter	50 mL
1/4 tsp	salt	1 mL
2 tbsp	flour	25 mL
1 cup	**PEI Milk**	250 mL
1	pkg (4 oz / 125 g) cream cheese	1
1/2 cup	Cheddar cheese grated	125 mL
1 cup	soft bread crumbs	250 mL

Cook vegetables in a small amount of water until tender. Drain and place in a 3 qt (3 L) casserole. In saucepan, melt half of butter. Blend in salt and flour. Stir in milk. Cook, stirring constantly until mixture comes to a boil and thickens. Remove from heat and stir in cream cheese until smooth. Pour sauce mixture over vegetables and mix lightly. Top with Cheddar cheese. Melt remaining butter; toss with bread crumbs and sprinkle on top of casserole. Bake at 350°F (180°C) for 20 minutes or until heated through. Makes 6-8 servings.

Photo: Victoria

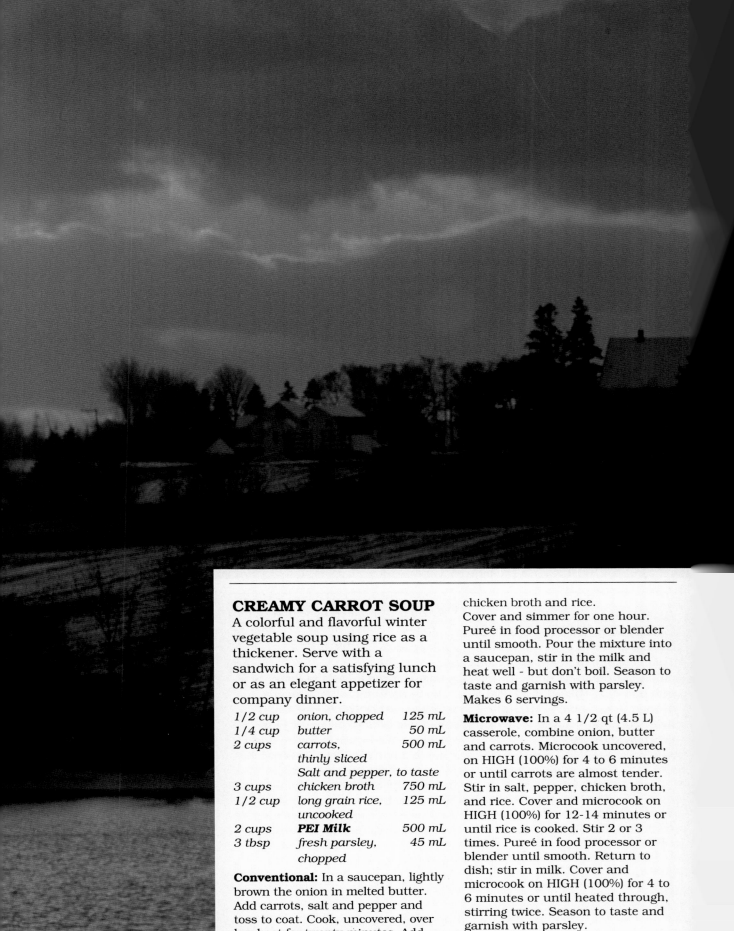

CREAMY CARROT SOUP

A colorful and flavorful winter vegetable soup using rice as a thickener. Serve with a sandwich for a satisfying lunch or as an elegant appetizer for company dinner.

1/2 cup	onion, chopped	125 mL
1/4 cup	butter	50 mL
2 cups	carrots, thinly sliced	500 mL
	Salt and pepper, to taste	
3 cups	chicken broth	750 mL
1/2 cup	long grain rice, uncooked	125 mL
2 cups	**PEI Milk**	500 mL
3 tbsp	fresh parsley, chopped	45 mL

Conventional: In a saucepan, lightly brown the onion in melted butter. Add carrots, salt and pepper and toss to coat. Cook, uncovered, over low heat for twenty minutes. Add chicken broth and rice.
Cover and simmer for one hour. Pureé in food processor or blender until smooth. Pour the mixture into a saucepan, stir in the milk and heat well - but don't boil. Season to taste and garnish with parsley. Makes 6 servings.

Microwave: In a 4 1/2 qt (4.5 L) casserole, combine onion, butter and carrots. Microcook uncovered, on HIGH (100%) for 4 to 6 minutes or until carrots are almost tender. Stir in salt, pepper, chicken broth, and rice. Cover and microcook on HIGH (100%) for 12-14 minutes or until rice is cooked. Stir 2 or 3 times. Pureé in food processor or blender until smooth. Return to dish; stir in milk. Cover and microcook on HIGH (100%) for 4 to 6 minutes or until heated through, stirring twice. Season to taste and garnish with parsley.

ALMOND COATED CHICKEN WITH ORANGE SAUCE

This creamy, delicate sauce on chicken breasts is delightfully enhanced by the almond and orange duo. Serve with fluffy mashed potatoes and a favorite green vegetable.

6	boneless, skinless chicken breast halves, flattened	6
	Flour (to coat chicken)	
2	eggs, beaten	2
1/2 cup	ground almonds	125 mL
1 tbsp	butter	15mL
1/4 cup	chopped onion	50 mL
2 tbsp	flour	25 mL
1/4 tsp	poultry seasoning	1 mL
1 1/2 cups	**PEI Milk**	375 mL
1/4 cup	orange marmalade	50 mL
1/2 tsp	grated orange rind	2 mL
1/4 cup	orange juice	50 mL
	Salt and pepper, to taste	

Coat chicken breasts in flour, then dip in eggs and roll in almonds. Bake at 400°F (200°C) for 18-20 minutes or until no longer pink inside. Melt butter in frypan and sauté onion until tender. Blend in flour and poultry seasoning. Gradually add milk. Cook and stir over medium heat until mixture boils and thickens. Remove from heat. Add marmalade, orange rind, orange juice and salt and pepper, to taste. To serve, pour the sauce over the chicken breasts. Makes 6 servings.

Photo: Park Corner

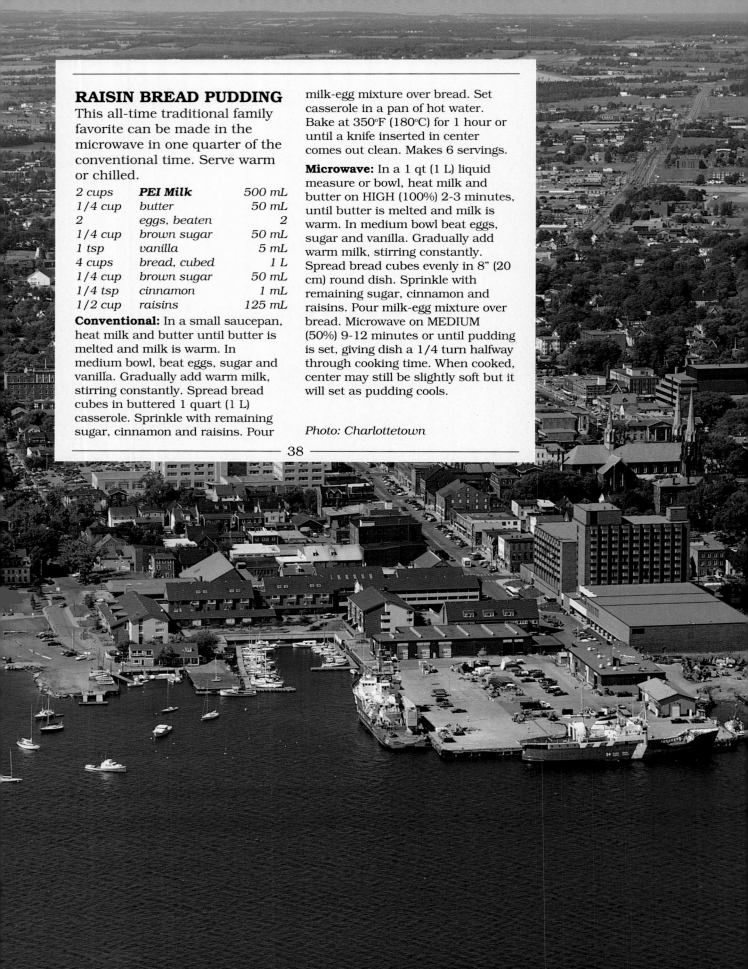

RAISIN BREAD PUDDING

This all-time traditional family favorite can be made in the microwave in one quarter of the conventional time. Serve warm or chilled.

2 cups	**PEI Milk**	500 mL
1/4 cup	butter	50 mL
2	eggs, beaten	2
1/4 cup	brown sugar	50 mL
1 tsp	vanilla	5 mL
4 cups	bread, cubed	1 L
1/4 cup	brown sugar	50 mL
1/4 tsp	cinnamon	1 mL
1/2 cup	raisins	125 mL

Conventional: In a small saucepan, heat milk and butter until butter is melted and milk is warm. In medium bowl, beat eggs, sugar and vanilla. Gradually add warm milk, stirring constantly. Spread bread cubes in buttered 1 quart (1 L) casserole. Sprinkle with remaining sugar, cinnamon and raisins. Pour milk-egg mixture over bread. Set casserole in a pan of hot water. Bake at 350°F (180°C) for 1 hour or until a knife inserted in center comes out clean. Makes 6 servings.

Microwave: In a 1 qt (1 L) liquid measure or bowl, heat milk and butter on HIGH (100%) 2-3 minutes, until butter is melted and milk is warm. In medium bowl beat eggs, sugar and vanilla. Gradually add warm milk, stirring constantly. Spread bread cubes evenly in 8" (20 cm) round dish. Sprinkle with remaining sugar, cinnamon and raisins. Pour milk-egg mixture over bread. Microwave on MEDIUM (50%) 9-12 minutes or until pudding is set, giving dish a 1/4 turn halfway through cooking time. When cooked, center may still be slightly soft but it will set as pudding cools.

Photo: Charlottetown

38

P.E.I. Hog Commodity Marketing Board

Lighten your fork with Pork

P.E.I. Cattlemen's Association

RED MEATS

For eons, meat has been enjoyed by homo sapiens as an important staple. It has been the mainstay of the diet due to its nutrient content, good value, convenience and great taste. In response to public demand, today's meat is leaner due to improved breeding and feeding techniques. Changes in the Canadian meat grading systems have encouraged the production of lean meat.

The meat industry is vital and dynamic and responds to consumers' needs. New products, new packaging and wider choices are the trend. Plus, convenient processed meats are showing up in the meat counter as "light" varieties, with reduced fat, calories and sodium.

As an added bonus, livestock are the best recyclers on earth. They convert material that cannot be used by other animals into high-quality protein in the form of meat and milk. The production of perennial forages, plants that are grown to feed livestock, is the solution to some environmental problems dealing with soil degradation, erosion, accumulation of salts and compaction.

TOURTIERE

The hog industry is as traditional on P.E.I. as "Tourtière". The Acadian meat pie contained chicken, rabbit, pork, or beef in combinations that varied from community to community and from cook to cook. Cooks then guarded their recipes but here is one you should pass on to others!

1 lb	lean ground **PEI Pork**	500 g
1/4 cup	onion, diced	50 mL
1	clove garlic, minced	1
1/2 tsp	salt	2 mL
1/2 tsp	summer savory	2 mL
1/4 tsp	celery salt	1 mL
1/4 tsp	ground cloves	1 mL
1/2 cup	water	125 mL
1/2 cup	bread crumbs	125 mL
	Pastry for 2-crust 9" (22.5 cm) pie	

Place pork, onion, garlic, salt, summer savory, celery salt, cloves and water in a saucepan. Bring to a boil, reduce heat and cook, uncovered, about 20 minutes or until half the liquid evaporates. Cover and cook 20 minutes longer. Remove from heat, add half the bread crumbs and let stand 10 minutes. If the fat is all absorbed by the bread do not add more. If not, add remaining crumbs. Cool. Line 9" (22.5 cm) pie plate with pastry, fill with meat mixture. Cover with top pastry. Bake in 400°F (200°C) oven 20-30 minutes or until lightly browned. Makes 6-8 servings.

Tip: Add 1 cup (250 mL) cooked mashed potatoes to cooked meat mixture in place of the bread crumbs.

Photo: Hope River

TERIYAKI PORK STEAKS

Serve pork steaks (chops) with rice or baked potato and your favorite colorful vegetable.

4 or 6	boneless, **PEI Pork** loin steaks or bone-in chops cut 1 - 11/2 inches (2.5 - 3.5 cm) thick	4 or 6
1/2 cup	orange juice	125 mL
1/4 cup	soy sauce	50 mL
1/4 cup	water	50 mL
2	cloves garlic, minced	2
2 tbsp	honey	25 mL
1/2 tsp	ground ginger	2 mL

Combine all ingredients except pork steaks (chops) in a non-metallic container. Stir well and add pork. Marinate for 2 hours at room temperature or overnight in the refrigerator. Remember, the longer the pork marinates, the better the flavour. Barbecue or broil for 8 to 10 minutes on each side or until steaks (chops) are still slightly pink inside and juices just run clear. Makes 4-6 servings.

Tip: If in a hurry, broil or barbecue unmarinated pork steaks (chops). While they are cooking, add 1 tbsp (15 mL) cornstarch to the sauce mixture and heat in saucepan or microwave. Pour over cooked steaks (chops) and serve immediately.

Photo: New Glasgow

BEEF WELLINGTON

For elegant holiday entertaining, put beef on the menu with this recipe. It is guaranteed to appeal to both the eye and the palate.

3 lbs	**PEI Beef** rib-eye or tenderloin roast	1.5 Kg
1/4 cup	butter	50 mL
2 cups	fresh mushroom slices	500 mL
1/4 cup	chopped onion	50 mL
1/4 cup	chopped parsley pastry, enough for two double-crust pies	50 mL
4 oz	liver sausage or liver paté	115 g
1	egg, beaten	1

Preheat oven to 425°F (220°C). Place beef on a rack in an open roasting pan and cook for 50 minutes or until meat thermometer registers 120°F (50°C). Remove from oven, let stand 30 minutes. Melt butter in a frypan, sauté mushrooms and onions until tender. Add parsley. Cook until all liquid evaporates. Cool. Roll pastry into a 18" x 14" (45 x 35 cm) rectangle, 1/4 inch (7mm) thick. Spread liver sausage or paté over the surface leaving a 2" (5 cm) thick margin around edges. Spoon mushroom mixture down center of pastry. Place roast top side down in the middle of the pastry. Wrap meat completely with pastry sealing edges with beaten egg. Decorate with extra pieces of pastry, cut with cookie cutters, if desired. Place roast "seam-side" down on baking sheet. Brush top and sides with egg. Cook at 425°F (220°C) for 30 minutes. Let cool 10 minutes before carving. Makes 6 to 8 servings.

Tip: This recipe may be completely prepared ahead of time and reheated at 300°F(150°C) for 45 - 60 minutes.

Tip: Save time by substituting one package of puff pastry, thawed, for the 2 double crust-pastries.

BEEF STIR FRY
Based on a recipe created by
Chef Ron Alain, Rodd Mill River
Resort

A quick and simple recipe for
those days when dinner has to
be on the table in a hurry. Serve
with fluffy mashed potatoes or
rice and a green salad.

1 lb	**PEI Beef** *tenderloin or sirloin steak, cut in strips*	500 g
1 tbsp	*vegetable oil*	15 mL
1	*clove garlic, minced*	1
1 tbsp	*fresh ginger root, peeled and grated*	15 mL
1/4 cup	*onion, cut in cubes*	50 mL
1/2 cup	*red wine or sherry*	125 mL
1 cup	*green pepper, cut in strips*	250 mL
1 cup	*mushrooms, sliced*	250 mL
1 cup	*broccoli florets*	250 mL
1 cup	*carrots, cut in julienne strips*	250 mL
1 tbsp	*cornstarch*	15 mL
1 cup	*beef broth*	250 mL
2 tbsp	*soy sauce*	25 mL

In wok or heavy skillet, sauté beef
strips in oil, over high heat, until
lightly browned. Add garlic, ginger
root, and onions and sauté for 1
minute. Reduce heat to medium.
Stir in red wine and vegetables;
cook for 3 to 4 minutes. Mix
cornstarch with beef broth and soy
sauce. Add to beef and vegetables.
Cook, stirring constantly until
sauce is thickened and bubbly.
Makes 4 servings.

HERB STUFFED LAMB CHOPS

The wonderful taste of lamb roasted in the oven! Entertain simply, yet elegantly with these delicious stuffed rib lamb chops.

8	double rib **PEI Lamb** chops (2 rib bones each chop)	8
1 cup	fresh coarse bread crumbs	250 mL
1/2 tsp	dried mint leaves or	2 mL
8	fresh mint leaves, chopped	8
1/2 tsp	basil	2 mL
1/4 tsp	rosemary	1 mL
4	cloves garlic, minced	4
1 tbsp	lemon juice	15 mL
	Salt and pepper, to taste	

Between ribs in each double rib chop, cut a pouch. Combine bread crumbs, mint, basil, rosemary, garlic, lemon juice, salt and pepper. Spoon the dressing into the cut. Place chops, stuffing side up in baking dish or broiler pan. Roast in 400°F (200°C) oven for 30 minutes for medium doneness. Turn broiler on at end of cooking period for 2 minutes to brown, and crisp top if necessary. Makes 4 servings.

Roasted potatoes and tender crisp broccoli complete your meal.

Tip: You may wish to use two "single" ribs per serving and hold the dressing in between with tooth picks.

Photo: Canoe Cove

SEAFOOD

Fishing for commercial gain on the Atlantic coast of Canada began when explorer John Cabot reached the Eastern shores of Newfoundland. When the struggle began between England and France for control of the "New World", it was not a struggle for gold or even fur - but for cod. Fortresses were built for the protection of this fishery.

A large percentage of early settlers who fished on Prince Edward Island also found part of their employment in agriculture. The reason for this switching of roles between farmer and fishermen was partially due to the Island's short fishing season created by ice conditions in winter.

Prince Edward Island is well known for its plentiful supply of quality seafood. Delicious lobsters, tender "Malpeque" oysters and plump "Island Blue" mussels are among the most famous.

Prince Edward Island also produces snow crab, rock crab, sea scallops, a variety of clams, cod, hake, flounder, redfish, herring, mackerel, smelts, eels and the giant Bluefin tuna. The aquaculture industry has diversified into bay scallops, Atlantic salmon and rainbow trout.

When preparing seafood it is important that it not be overcooked. For moist, flavorful results cook seafood at a high temperature for a short period of time.

MARINATED MUSSELS

Based on a recipe by Chef Perry Bowers, Rodd Brudenell Resort.

1/2 cup	vegetable oil	125 mL
1/3 cup	vinegar	75 mL
1/4 cup	dry white wine	50 mL
2 tbsp	lemon juice	25 mL
1 tsp	dill paste (or 1/4 tsp/1 mL dill seed crushed)	5 mL
1/2 tsp	thyme	2 mL
1	bay leaf	1
	Salt and pepper, to taste	
1 lb	cooked **Island Blue Mussel** meat (3 lbs/1.5 kg. fresh mussels)	500 g
1	small onion, thinly sliced	1
1	small green pepper, thinly sliced	1
1	small red pepper, thinly sliced	1

Combine oil, vinegar, wine and lemon juice; mix well. Stir in dill, thyme, bay leaf, salt and pepper; mix well. Add mussel meat and vegetables. Store in a covered container in the refrigerator for at least 12 hours before serving.

Tip: Create an unforgettable luncheon or buffet salad by tossing Marinated Mussels with your favorite cold cooked pasta.

Photo: Oyster Fishing, Wilmot Bay

OYSTER CHOWDER

This chowder makes a tasty treat all year round.

24	shucked **Malpeque Oysters** with liquor	24
1/4 cup	butter	50 mL
1/4 cup	onion, chopped	50 mL
1/4 cup	celery, chopped	50 mL
1 tbsp	flour	15 mL
1 1/2 cups	water	375 mL
2 cups	potatoes, diced	500 mL
2 cups	milk	500 mL
1 tsp	salt	5 mL
1/2 tsp	pepper	2 mL
1 tbsp	fresh parsley, chopped	15 mL

Poach the oysters in their liquor for about 4 to 5 minutes or until edges begin to curl. Drain oysters, reserving juice; set aside. Sauté onion and celery in butter until tender. Add flour and gradually stir in water and oyster liquor. Add potatoes and simmer until tender. Stir in milk, oysters, salt and pepper. Heat gently, cook until smooth. Garnish with parsley. Makes 4 servings.

Photo: Victoria

DELUXE CRAB DIP

A welcome addition to any buffet, this dip can be served with fresh vegetables or crackers.

3/4 cup	**PEI Crab** meat (Snow or Rock Crab)	175 mL
1	pkg (8 oz/228 g) cream cheese, softened	1
1/2 cup	mayonnaise	125 mL
2 tbsp	ketchup	25 mL
3 tbsp	French dressing	45 mL
1 tbsp	finely chopped onion	15 mL

Drain crab meat; remove any bits of shell or cartilage. Break into small pieces. Blend cream cheese, mayonnaise, ketchup, French dressing, and onion until smooth. Add crab and mix well. Chill several hours. Makes 2 cups (500 mL).

Photo: Trout Fishing, East Royalty

VICTORIA FISH ROLLS

Elegant and scrumptious, perfect for those special dinners.

l lb	**PEI Cod, Sole**, or **Hake** fillets	500 g
1	pkg (11 oz/300 g) frozen chopped broccoli, thawed	1
2 cups	cooked rice	500 mL
1/4 cup	butter	50 mL
1/4 cup	flour	50 mL
1/2 tsp	salt	2 mL
dash	pepper	dash
2 cups	milk	500 mL
2 tbsp	lemon juice	25 mL
1/2 cup	grated Cheddar cheese	125 mL

If fillets are thick, slice diagonally to make thin fillets. Combine broccoli and rice. Place 1 tbsp (15 mL) broccoli/rice mixture on each fillet and roll up. Spread remaining mixture in greased baking dish. Arrange fish rolls on top of rice.

Make white sauce by melting butter and stirring in flour, salt and pepper. Gradually stir in milk. Cook over low heat until thickened. Stir in lemon juice. Pour sauce over fish and rice. Sprinkle with grated cheese. Bake in 425°F (220°C) oven for 30 minutes. Makes 6 servings.

Photo: North Lake

BACON WRAPPED SCALLOPS

A definite favorite.

1 lb	**PEI Scallops**	500 g
1/4 cup	vegetable oil	50 mL
2 tbsp	lemon juice	25 mL
1 tsp	salt	5 mL
dash	white pepper	dash
1/2 lb	bacon	250 g
	Paprika	

Marinate scallops in oil, lemon juice, salt and pepper for 30 minutes, stirring occasionally. Partially cook bacon and cut each slice in half crosswise. Remove scallops from sauce, reserving sauce for basting. Wrap each scallop in a piece of bacon and secure with a toothpick. Baste with sauce and broil for 5 minutes. Turn, baste with sauce and sprinkle with paprika. Broil an additional 5 to 7 minutes or until bacon is crisp and scallop is opaque. Makes 30 appetizers.

PRINCE EDWARD ISLAND PRESERVE CO.

Prince Edward Island Preserve Co. Inc.
Bruce MacNaughton
New Glasgow, Hunter River RR #2
P.E.I. C0A 1N0 (902) 964-2524

For those who like good quality food, a visit to this preserve factory and shop is a "must." Not only can visitors watch Canada's finest preserves being produced, but also sit and enjoy home baked goods, gourmet coffee and over 20 imported teas. Located right in the scenic village of New Glasgow.

FRUITS / VEGETABLES

Serve them in soups, stews and salads. Serve them hot or cold, cooked or fresh! From appetizers to desserts - or anywhere in between.

Fruits and vegetables add variety to our meals and our diets. They provide many vitamins and minerals, are virtually fat free, low in calories, are good sources of carbohydrates and fiber, and naturally low in sodium.

Cole crops - cabbage, broccoli, Brussels sprouts - thrive in the Island's sandy loam soil and cool, moist climate. Rutabagas, carrots and parsnips all flourish in the rich, well-drained soil.

Strawberries and blueberries are the most important fruit crops grown on Prince Edward Island. Small amounts of apples and raspberries are also produced.

There is potential for further development and expansion in the production of fruits and vegetables on Prince Edward Island. Many of the crops can be grown economically on relatively small land areas.

FRESH STRAWBERRY PIE

No one has experienced paradise on earth until they have eaten fully ripe and luscious strawberries, warmed by Island sunshine.

1 quart	**PEI Strawberries**, sliced	1 L
1/2 cup	water	125 mL
3 tbsp	cornstarch	45 mL
1 cup	sugar	250 mL
1 tsp	lime juice	5 mL
1 cup	whipping cream	250 mL

Reserve 1 cup (250 mL) berries. Place the rest in baked Butter Pecan Pie Crust (recipe follows). Mash reserved berries. Simmer with water for 5 minutes. Remove from heat. Combine cornstarch and sugar, then add to fruit. Stir. Return to heat. Cook slowly until juice is thick and clear, stirring constantly. Cool slightly. Add lime juice; pour over berries in the pie shell. Chill. Whip cream. Serve pie topped with whipped cream.

Butter Pecan Pie Crust

1/2 cup	butter	125 mL
1 cup	flour	250 mL
1/4 cup	brown sugar	50 mL
1/3 cup	chopped pecans	75 mL

Blend butter, flour and sugar until crumbs form. Stir in nuts. Press gently into 9" (22.5 cm) pie plate. Bake at 375°F (190°C) for 12 to 15 minutes until golden brown.

Photo: Tryon

SPECTACULAR STRAWBERRY CAKE

Bring the summer taste of berries to your guests all year round with this party dessert.

1	pkg angel food cake mix	1
1	pkg (3 oz/85 g) strawberry gelatin	1
1 1/4 cups	crushed **PEI Strawberries**, fresh or frozen	300 mL
4 cups	vanilla ice cream, softened	1 L
1 cup	whipping cream	250 mL
2 tbsp	sugar	25 mL
1/2 tsp	vanilla	2 mL

Bake angel food cake according to package directions. Cool. Tear cake into bite size pieces. Heat strawberry gelatin and crushed strawberries in saucepan to dissolve gelatin. Add ice cream, stir until well-blended. In angel food pan, make three layers of cake and strawberry mixture. Pat down each layer with spoon. Refrigerate overnight. At serving time whip cream, beat in sugar and vanilla. Turn cake out on serving plate. Frost with cream and garnish with strawberries. Makes 12 - 15 servings.

Photo: Old Home Week Harness Racing, Charlottetown

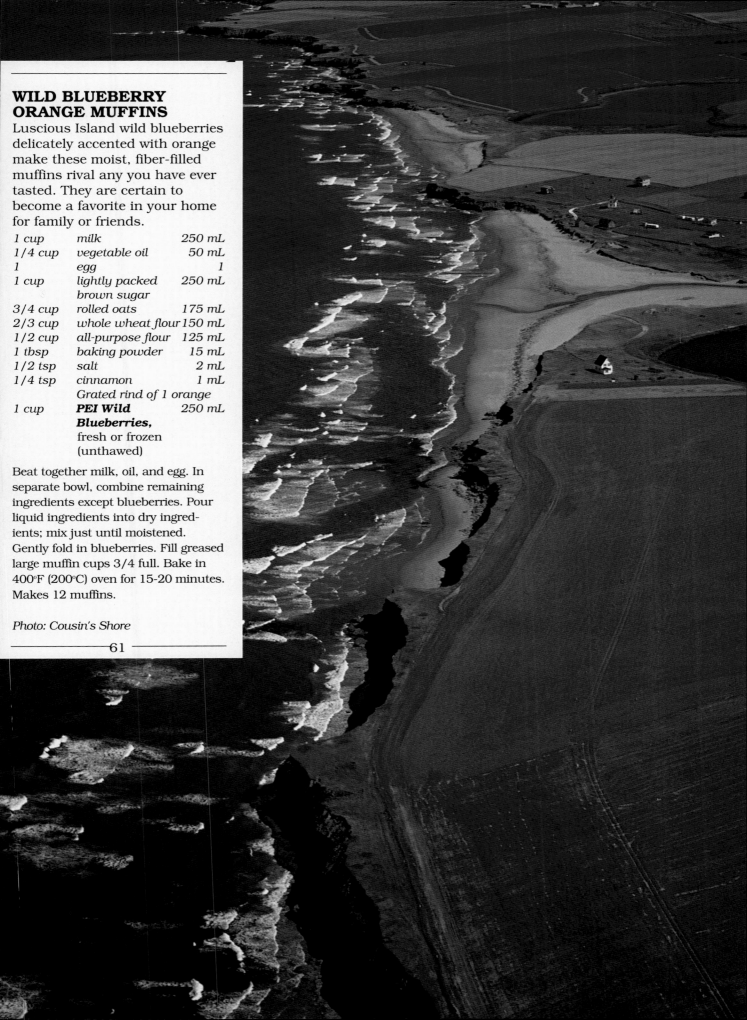

WILD BLUEBERRY ORANGE MUFFINS

Luscious Island wild blueberries delicately accented with orange make these moist, fiber-filled muffins rival any you have ever tasted. They are certain to become a favorite in your home for family or friends.

1 cup	milk	250 mL
1/4 cup	vegetable oil	50 mL
1	egg	1
1 cup	lightly packed brown sugar	250 mL
3/4 cup	rolled oats	175 mL
2/3 cup	whole wheat flour	150 mL
1/2 cup	all-purpose flour	125 mL
1 tbsp	baking powder	15 mL
1/2 tsp	salt	2 mL
1/4 tsp	cinnamon	1 mL
	Grated rind of 1 orange	
1 cup	**PEI Wild Blueberries,** fresh or frozen (unthawed)	250 mL

Beat together milk, oil, and egg. In separate bowl, combine remaining ingredients except blueberries. Pour liquid ingredients into dry ingredients; mix just until moistened. Gently fold in blueberries. Fill greased large muffin cups 3/4 full. Bake in 400°F (200°C) oven for 15-20 minutes. Makes 12 muffins.

Photo: Cousin's Shore

61

HONEY'D RUTABAGA AND CARROTS

Honey is cherished by cooks for its remarkable keeping qualities and the unique texture and golden color it gives to other foods.

1 1/2 cups	**PEI Rutabaga**, cubed	375 mL
4	medium **PEI Carrots**, peeled, sliced	4
3 tbsp	butter	45 mL
2 tbsp	**PEI Honey**	25 mL
1/4 tsp	salt	1 mL
pinch	cinnamon	pinch
pinch	nutmeg	pinch

In small amount of boiling water cook rutabaga and carrots until tender crisp. Drain. Add butter, honey, salt, cinnamon and nutmeg. Cook over low heat, stirring until sauce thickens and vegetables are coated. Makes 6 servings.

RASPBERRY MERINGUE TORTE

This sensational raspberry dessert is easy to prepare and perfect for entertaining.

Meringue:

pinch	salt	pinch
pinch	cream of tartar	pinch
4	egg whites at room temperature	4
1 cup	sugar	250 mL
1 tsp	vanilla	5 mL
1/2 cup	ground filberts, or other nuts	125 mL
1/2 cup	ground almonds	125 mL

Filling and Icing:

2 cups	whipping cream	500 mL
1/3 cup	icing sugar	75 mL
1/2 tsp	vanilla	2 mL
1 cup	**PEI Raspberries**, fresh or frozen	250 mL
1/3 cup	finely chopped filberts	75 mL

Meringue: Butter two 8" (20 cm) layer pans. Dust with flour and line with circles of wax paper cut to fit. Sprinkle salt and cream of tartar over the egg whites. Beat at slow speed until foamy, then increase speed to high and beat to soft peaks. Still beating, add the sugar gradually; continue beating until meringue stands in stiff peaks. Fold in the vanilla, ground filberts and almonds. Spoon into prepared pans. Bake in 350°F (180°C) oven 30-35 minutes or until evenly browned. Remove the layers from pans and cool thoroughly on racks. Peel off the paper.

Filling and Icing: Whip the cream to firm peaks. Sweeten with icing sugar and vanilla. Reserve half of whipped cream. Fold raspberries into the remaining whipped cream. Spread cream-fruit mixture over one layer of cake. Top with second layer. Ice cake with reserved whipped cream; sprinkle with chopped filberts. Makes 8-10 servings.

Tip: Meringue layers may be made 3 to 4 days in advance and stored in an airtight container.

Photo: Along the Kings Byway Drive

SUPER COLESLAW

A honey version of the ever-popular coleslaw.

1	medium head	1
	PEI Cabbage	
1-2	**PEI Carrots**	1-2
1/2	green pepper	1/2
1	onion	1
1	stalk celery	1
1 tsp	salt	5 mL
1 cup	vinegar	250 mL
2/3 cup	**PEI Honey**	150 mL
2/3 cup	vegetable oil	150 mL

Grate or finely chop vegetables. Bring to a boil salt, vinegar, honey and oil. Pour over vegetables and toss to mix well. Refrigerate for at least one day before serving. Makes 10-12 servings.

Photo: Cavendish

TRADITIONAL RODD HOSPITALITY

With six locations on the Island, we can offer you a variety of dining experiences...from fine white linen dining to dinner theatre, to hearty 'down home' fare.

Fresh Island seafoods, garden produce, and delectable desserts are just some of the treats we have in store for you.

The Charlottetown -
A Rodd Classic Hotel
Charlottetown, 894-7371

Rodd Royalty Inn
Charlottetown, 894-8566

Rodd Confederation Inn & Suites
Charlottetown, 892-2481

Rodd Brudenell River Resort
Roseneath, 652-2332

Rodd Mill River Resort
Woodstock, 859-3555

Loyalist Country Inn
Affiliated with Rodd Hotels & Resorts
Summerside, 436-3333

Rodd
HOTELS & RESORTS